Chappaquiddick Lullaby
a song of
Martha's Vineyard

Song & Story by Stacy Elizabeth Hall

Published by Island Moon Press · Oaks, PA

*Includes CD by Kate Taylor & Taylor Brown · Illustrated by Judith Pfeiffer

Stacy Elizabeth Hall dedicates this book

To Isabel Engley, who believed Chappy Song should be a book
and persuaded me to believe it too;

Steve, Katama and Zak Martellucci, my sailors and fishers,
who make my most precious memories,

Judy Pfeiffer who transforms them to live so gloriously on paper;

Claire Nickerson-Hall and Sonny Hall, my parents,
who are always there for me;

And in memory of my grandmother,
Marie Ruth Brown Nickerson Birch Kent
who wanted Katama and Zak to always have Chappy.
They would never have had it without you.

Chappaquiddick Lullaby
Chappy Song

By Stacy Elizabeth Hall

Text/Lyrics copyright 2007 by Stacy Hall Martellucci

Illustration copyright 2007 by Judith Pfeiffer

Book design and layout by Meghan J. Shupe

Production design by Island Moon Press

ISBN (13)   978-0-9755605-1-8
ISBN (10)   0-9755605-1-4
LCCN/PCN pending
Printed in China

Published by **Island Moon Press** · PO Box 956 · Oaks, PA 19456-0956 · 1 - 8 7 7 - 2 - K A T A M A · *www.IslandMoonPress.com*

Judith Pfeiffer dedicates this book

To Stacy, my muse. Thank you. I've been waiting a long time for you to find me and allow me to paint your wonderful word pictures.
It took a while but sometimes Serendipity can and does finally happen. Did I say "thank you"?

Also to my Derby guys, Hans and Christopher, for schooling me about all of the fishies swimming through these pages.
And to my sailor boy, Jonathan, who also loves and respects the sea.
Finally to Lynn-y, the sweetest fish of all.

Can you find the Wampum?

Wampum

Kate Taylor, Judy Pfeiffer and Stacy Hall all love wampum. Judy has hidden a piece of wampum on each page. Look carefully for the purple and white shell.

What is Wampum?

Wampum is the Algonquian word for the purple and white cylindrical beads made from the shell of the quohaug. This relative of the clam grows on the eastern shores of Long Island, NY extending northeastward to Cape Cod, MA including the islands of Martha's Vineyard and Nantucket. Wampum was used as a means of communication by the tribal peoples of the northeastern United States as the beads were woven into belts and strung into message strands. The symbols formed by these beads documented important events, treaties, marriages, and invitations and aided the great oral traditions of these Indian communities. As European settlers began to colonize what was for them a new world, they too manufactured wampum and traded it with the native people for fur, use of land and other things. Wampum gradually became a medium of exchange for all kinds of goods and services. Parliament put a pound value on wampum and with it you could, for example, pay your Massachusetts state taxes and your tuition at Harvard College. Eventually, the traditional native uses for wampum disappeared as their culture was overcome by colonization, and the settlers reverted to coinage for their economic transactions. The craft of wampum bead making lay dormant for a century or more. In 1970, Charlie Witham, Joan Lelacheur and I realized that the beautiful ocean tumbled shell pieces we found on the shores of our island home were of the same material as the beads we had seen in Native American collections in museums. Through research of the traditional uses of wampum and its manufacture, we were able to revive this historic bead. - Kate Taylor

Close your eyes, close your eyes
And dream the whole night long.

Close your eyes, close your eyes
Chappy holds you in her arms.

Close your eyes, close your eyes

She'll keep you safe from harm.

Listen to the wind and waves,

Hear the Chappaquiddick Song!

RAIN, RAIN, GO AWAY

The house is snug against spring storms

Though the northeasters will blow.

Your bed is warm, just close your eyes
The wind sings a song just so.

You're clean and rosy brown with sun
From playing through a beach day,
You're drowsy now from that salt air
Let the sandman take you away.

Feel the warm night air blow sweetly in

As it comes down Katama Bay.

Island Moon
Edgartown

Let the sound carry you away.

Boats bob softly at their moorings

And as you sleep, let your spirit rise, take a trip down the Milky Way.

Soar high out o'er Wasque Point
Let the bluefish show you the way.

Ride on up the isle to the old carousel
Where your fish becomes a Flying Horse.
When you catch the brass ring your free ride will bring
You home to Chappy to sing...

Close your eyes, close your eyes
And dream the whole night long.
Close your eyes, close your eyes
Chappy holds you in her arms.

Close your eyes, close your eyes
She'll keep you safe from harm.
Listen to the wind and waves,
Hear the Chappaquiddick Song!

Chappy Song

Wait a minute... frogs like rain!

Pinkie Tinks

Remember that day when the clouds filled the sky

And we wanted to go to the bay?

Grammie gave you some brooms and then just before noon

You had swept all the clouds all away!

Imagine the bay where our work becomes play
As we gather some steamers for lunch.
We're all having fun up to elbows in mud
As the dog adds a clam to the bunch!

And then oh! there's a blitz and we're into the fish
Oh baby oh baby we'll say!
Dad catches a blue almost bigger than you
Oh Daddy oh Daddy hooray!

Later that day just back from the bay
We'll check our cocoons with wide eyes.
No longer all green there's a monarch with wings
That sits on your hand as it dries!

Larva

Chrysalis

Monarch

ON TIME III EDGARTOWN

Sand dollars for beach candy

Oh Daddy oh Daddy oh baby I hope you catch some fi...
Oh Daddy oh Daddy oh baby That's my fishy fishiest wish
Oh - oh - oh - oh - ho ho
Oh - oh - oh - oh - oh - ho ha !

In the evening we'll take that great monster fish
On the ferry to town to be weighed.
Dad's name on the list we'll give him a kiss,
When we're home on Chappy I'll say...

I remember when you said, "Nigh-nigh boaps,"
Instead of "Goodnight Boats."

You're growing straight and strong, my love, your life is all I could hope.

Now I'll tuck you safely in your bed
And listen to your prayers,
And I'll say a prayer that's all my own,
Thanking God you're in our care.

Close your eyes, close your eyes
And dream the whole night long.
Close your eyes, close your eyes
Chappy holds you in her arms.

Close your eyes, close your eyes
She'll keep you safe from harm.
Listen to the wind and waves,

Hear the Chappaquiddick Song!

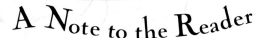

A Note to the Reader

Chappaquiddick, ("Chappy") which is said to mean "Separated Island," is part of Edgartown on Martha's Vineyard, which lies off the coast of Cape Cod in southeastern Massachusetts.

Reachable only by boat and (sometimes) by four-wheel-drive vehicle, Chappaquiddick is a sparkling, magical isle. In September and October of every year, it is a prime fishing destination for those that compete in the Martha's Vineyard Striped Bass & Bluefish Derby. The Trustees of Reservations manage a most beautiful part of the island, beloved of fishers, birders, clammers and beach babies of all ages, called Wasque ("way-squee"). It is a place of expedition, abundant wildlife, and natural wonder.

For many years, my family owned two little houses, the North and South Cottages, perched on a bluff overlooking Edgartown Harbor on Chappaquiddick. Our home was surrounded by miraculous mornings, glittery vistas, breath-taking sunsets, sweetly scented wildflowers, and incredible stars. The Milky Way is amazingly clear there, a vaulted highway of light. It is also a place of misty, mysterious mornings, sudden clearings, and horizontally raining northeasters.

I wrote *Chappy Song* in the fall of 1992. We knew that due to my grandmother's recent death, our island paradise might have to be sold. Although we owned those houses for many more years, knowing that we might lose them heightened my awareness of how truly enchanting and healing it was to be there, to call it home. I appreciated how lucky I was. I treasured every moment. I took endless pictures and videos. It became a family joke when I would take off with my camera that, "Stacy's saying good-bye again." And I would always cry.

I sang the *Chappy Song* at bedtime for many years, especially to my daughter, Katama, who still never wants to go to sleep. But there comes a day when your children beg you not to sing, especially in public. With my children so grown up, I realize what mothers have been telling me for years—it's very quick. Don't miss it. Make as many memories as you can. Explore magical places. Take lots of pictures. Sing while you can!

In 2004, I published my first book, *The Legend of Katama*. The thing about a first book is that everyone assumes there will be a second. My mentoring friend, Isabel Engley, asked (repeatedly) "What about the *Chappy Song*? It would make a great book." Over a year's time, she continued to sing the song's praises and after awhile, I figured I could at least take a look at some illustrators. When Judy Pfeiffer answered my ad in the *Martha's Vineyard Times* and became really excited about the project, it seemed to take on a life of its own. Then Kate Taylor and Taylor Brown said that they'd be happy to sing *Chappy Song*, and amazingly enough, with a lot of help from family and friends, Isabel's idea becomes an actual book, a real song and a CD!

Chappaquiddick Lullaby is an ode to an island home and a love song to my family. If you live on Martha's Vineyard, I hope it will remind you of home; and if you are visiting, I hope it will resonate with some of your memories of your trip. I also hope that it will remind each reader of their own beach days and nights – and if it helps you to get your children to sleep, it's all good. My work here is done!

Stacy Hall Martellucci, M. Ed. · Edgartown, Massachusetts · February 2006

The author would like to thank

Judy Pfeiffer, *artiste extraordinaire*, who took a song and some memories and made the most magical pictures. Working with you has been complete bliss. Kate Taylor, elegant and gracious, who patiently listened to me babble and decided to work with me anyway. Your participation in this project is an honor for me. Taylor Brown, whose talent and enthusiasm are matched by his professionalism. Gordon Millsaps, excellent and fun to be with sound engineer. Rigel Byrum-Ridge, for lending an atmospherically musical hand. Thanks guys, for taking my tune and making it a real song and CD. Meghan Shupe, Kevin Link and Andrew Ward, my production team. Thank you for your meticulously produced product. Working with all of you is such a treat. And a relief!

Ann Bassett, of the *Bunch of Grapes*, who kindly supports my work and helps whenever and wherever she can. Your expertise and island eye are invaluable. Annie McKenzie and Alan Crossland for the Katama photo shoot. Summer Sundays at Camp Anne are the best. Thanks for giving me rest and keeping me on track. Carol VanderVeer for her critical eye and edit. Carly Conway, her mom, Kim, and her grandmother Claire, who shared my initial excitement and realized that it would make a great coloring book. Bridget Tobin, who keeps me laughing. Laurel Whitaker for marketing support—thanks for offering to do what I hate to do! We'll be doing this for you soon! Elizabeth Germain, incredible chef, for delicious sustenance and rest. Chris Scott of the *Martha's Vineyard Preservation Trust* and John Custer of the *Martha's Vineyard Striped Bass and Bluefish Derby*, for kind permissions. Sharon Kelly at the *The Secret Garden*, Susan Mercier and David Le Breton at *Edgartown Books*, Zoe Pechter and Peter Economou at *Riley's Reads*, and Holly Nadler at *Sunporch Books*, thanks for selling my books and getting excited about them! Jean Bryant and Carol Fligor for all your help. Bobby Love for frisbee and dog collar. Todd Martin for CD 101. Becca Flint and Marcia Saunders for voice coaching. Sandy Hicks for the art of the deal. Sally Lodge for her expert opinion and time. Erin and Tony Geyelin for their help on matters contractual. And to Philip Craig and Shirley Prada Craig for being so very kind to me.

My sister-in-law Diane Martellucci Klein, for keeping Island Moon Press up and running, and always helping where ever she can. If it wasn't for your Chappy visit and request for beach weather, we might never have learned about cloud-sweeping! My sister-in-law, Karen Trudel Martellucci, for endless emotional and spiritual support. I don't know what I'd do without you. (And everyone at GMI for technical support.) My sister-in-law Amy Hall, for your constant excitement, caring, and co-production of Hall family events. I so appreciate how you all listen to me snivel and encourage me to keep going. And Abraham-Hicks for teaching me so much. Life **is** supposed to be fun!

My beautiful daughter, Katama Marie Martellucci, my Island girl, who can be counted on to catch the mistakes and calmly rescue the sailors. If it wasn't for you, there would've been no reason to sing lullabies in the first place. You *have* grown straight and strong, my love. I am so proud of you. My gorgeous son, Zak Martellucci, the Golden Boy, who, with his sister's help, transformed a tune into actual sheet music, also works carefully and patiently with wampum, and cheerfully carries boxes of books. You are a bright light in every life you touch, especially mine. My Mom and Dad, Claire Nickerson-Hall and Sonny Hall, for always caring about my dreams and helping me achieve them. Thanks, Mom, for teaching us about our islands, cloud-sweeping, and butterflies, and still always giving us a clean and beautiful place to call home. Thanks for listening to me cry and your sharp editorial eye. Dad, I know that you keep hoping that I'll get a "real" job, but thanks for being supportive of me anyway!

My excellent, patient, outdoorsman husband ("Daddy-oh-Baby") Steve Martellucci, who is always up for an adventure, even if it means another book. Your steadfast support allows me the space and time to create. Thank you for everything.

Isabel and Earle Engley, for having me as one of the "daughters," opening your homes to me and mine, and making the best salads. Without Isabel, this would just still be a song that I used to sing.

It takes a village. Thank you for being mine. I love you all.

Stacy Hall Martellucci, M.Ed. · Mont Clare, Pennsylvania · February 2006

About the Author

Stacy Elizabeth Hall, M. Ed., loves to be the Visiting Author at schools, libraries, and aquariums. She enjoys teaching about writing, publishing, following dreams, and the importance of intrinsic motivation in education. She lives with her family and black lab, Cala; and runs her publishing company, *Island Moon Press. Chappaquiddick Lullaby* is her second book. Her first book, *The Legend of Katama, The Creation Story of Dolphins, A Wampanoag Legend of Martha's Vineyard* was first published in 2004. Stacy loves to hear from readers and educators through her website at *www.IslandMoonPress.com.*

About the Illustrator

Judith Pfeiffer is an illustrator who lives and works on Martha's Vineyard. She is fond of all the colors but is partial to blue—specifically periwinkle blue. She also likes the word Pinkletink...Periwinkles and Pinkletinks, Oh My! Her email address is *JudithPfeiffer@adelphia.net.*

About the Musicians

Kate Taylor is a singer and songwriter whose first record, *Sister Kate* was released in 1970. It didn't sell a million copies but it should have. She went on to make two more albums in the 1970's; *Kate Taylor* and *It's in There and It's Got to Come Out.* She made the island of Martha's Vineyard her home, started her family and continued to write songs and perform, although her home life and her children were her first priority. While her daughters were young she helped revive the craft of wampum bead making. For ten years Kate served on the school committee of her town, Gay Head, Massachusetts. She spent several winters dredging the island's bay scallops off the floor of Menemsha Pond. In 2003 she released her fourth album, *Beautiful Road.* In 2005 she released *Kate Taylor Live at The Cutting Room.* She now performs in New York City and elsewhere. She is on a first name basis with her friend Sid Bernstein, the man who first brought the Beatles to America. Sid says he'd have Kate on the Ed Sullivan Show three Sundays in a row if only the show still existed. Her website is *www.KateTaylor.com.*

Taylor Brown is a Quaker-raised Philadelphia native who has been writing and performing songs since early childhood. He received a BA in music from Vassar College in 2006 and has released three albums including Taylor Brown Trio's *Notebook* (2005). Taylor has been recording and playing throughout the country with Kate Taylor since 2003. He can be reached through his website at *www.TaylorBrownMusic.net.*